DUMFRIES AND GALLOWAY'S LAST DAYS OF STEAM

by
W.A.C. Smith

On a wet 23 May 1960, Jubilee 4-6-0 No. 45663, 'Jervis', a London Midland Region locomotive shedded at Manchester Patricroft, stands at Nethercleugh with the 1.50 p.m. up 'Parly' from Glasgow Central to Carlisle, a train which called at most of the twenty-eight stations en route. It derived its nickname from parliamentary legislation of 1844 which compelled all British passenger railways to run at least one train daily, calling at every station, and travelling at not less than 12 m.p.h. with enclosed vehicles provided with seats. Fares were also not to exceed one penny per mile. Although largely superseded by a Cheap Trains Act in 1883, the name 'Parly' lived on among railwaymen. Three weeks after this photograph was taken Nethercleugh was one of six wayside stations on the Caledonian main line closed to passengers.

ISBN 1 84033 234 4

THE PUBLISHERS REGRET THAT THEY CANNOT SUPPLY
COPIES OF ANY PICTURES FEATURED IN THIS BOOK.

Photographed on 29 July 1961, Black Five 4-6-0 No. 45411 calls at Beattock with the 7.35 a.m. service from Aberdeen to Manchester. It was from this station, described in contemporary press reports as being of 'early English' style and 'tastefully decorated with flags', that on 9 September 1847 the directors of the Caledonian Railway made the first trip to Carlisle and back, being regaled with a sumptuous collation upon their return. The station survived until 1972; but under a more enlightened management than that provided by the Scottish Region of British Railways, it could have been retained as a railhead served by the new electric trains which were introduced in 1974.

INTRODUCTION

Although Dumfries and Galloway comprises the entire south-west corner of Scotland, as regards railways, it is traversed today only by the electrified West Coast main line (with Lockerbie being the only station), the Nith Valley route through Dumfries, and the straggling Stranraer branch from Girvan. However, prior to the Beeching cuts of the 1960s, there was a third main line, albeit a mainly single track one, which ran from Dumfries to Stranraer, while until 1921 the Solway Junction Railway bridged the Solway estuary at Annan. There was also a spread of rural branch lines, all long gone, and a useful cross-country link from Lockerbie to Dumfries.

The Caledonian Railway was first on the scene, opening their line from Carlisle to Edinburgh and Glasgow in 1848, with the formidable ten mile Beattock bank a noteworthy feature. Two years later the Nith Valley route gave the newly-formed Glasgow & South Western Railway access to Carlisle by means of running powers over the Caledonian line from Gretna Junction, and in 1862 the Portpatrick Railway (the 'Port Road') was completed from Castle Douglas, being joined fifteen years later at Challoch Junction, six miles east of Stranraer, by a railway from Girvan. In 1885 the Portpatrick Railway, which had been worked by the Caledonian Railway, was reconstituted as the Portpatrick & Wigtownshire Joint Railways.

The Solway Junction Railway was a grandiose scheme, backed by the Caledonian, which had come to fruition in 1869, but foundered as early as 1921 when its mile-long viaduct across the Solway was put out of use. The Kirtlebridge to Annan section, however, retained a passenger service until its withdrawal by the London, Midland & Scottish Railway in 1931.

Somewhat ironically, in view of the poor timekeeping on today's privatised system, the Caledonian Railway liked to call itself the 'True to Time Line'! However, it may also be remembered that the Caledonian held the unenviable distinction of having Britain's worst ever rail disaster which occurred on 22 May 1915 when 226 persons, mostly soldiers from the 7th Battalion The Royal Scots, died in a double collision at Quintinshill, a short distance north of the Gretna Junction.

The government-inspired Railway Grouping of 1923 put all

No. 44767, one of the ubiquitous Black Fives of an LMS design dating back to 1934, leaves Beattock on 31 July 1965 with an 0910 relief from Southport to Glasgow Central (the twenty-four hour clock was introduced to timetables on 14 June 1965).

lines in Dumfries and Galloway under control of the newly-formed London, Midland & Scottish Railway, excepting for a few miles of the Langholm branch which, as North British property, passed to the London & North Eastern Railway.

In both world wars there were extensive rail-served munitions factories at Gretna and Eastriggs on the Solway shore, and in 1941 the Cairnryan Military Railway was created to serve an emergency port on Loch Ryan. In 1943, as a 'wartime measure', the LMS withdrew the passenger service from Dumfries to Moniave over the former G&SW Cairn Valley Light Railway and it was never reinstated.

The nationalised British Railways came into being on 1 January 1948 and soon its Scottish Region was giving a foretaste of the Beeching axe with closures which started in 1950 with a short stretch of the Port Road from Stranraer to Portpatrick (the latter place having long since been demoted to the status of a very minor branch terminus from its original role of cross-channel port), along with the Whithorn branch from Newton Stewart and followed in 1952 by the Lockerbie to Dumfries line. The only other Caledonian branch in Dumfriesshire (apart from a short stretch of the Leadhills & Wanlockhead Light Railway) was the two mile link from Beattock to the small spa town of Moffat and this was axed in 1954.

In 1955 came the government-funded Modernisation Plan which resulted in several large, but short-lived, marshalling yards such as that at

Carlisle Kingmoor, and a hurried scramble to replace steam traction with diesel locomotives which subsequently were frequently found to give inferior performance. It was, perhaps, symbolic of the future that 1955 also brought a seventeen day strike by members of the ASLEF union which achieved little other than the alienation of customers who had previously sent considerable quantities of freight by rail.

Under the Beeching regime closures resumed in 1964 with the Langholm branch, while closure of the Kirkcudbright branch in 1965 preceded by a mere six weeks the disappearance of the Port Road, despite the latter being a potentially valuable asset in view of an upsurge in Irish traffic. The closure took place on 12 June when Black Fives Nos. 45480 and 44689 left Stranraer Harbour Station with the 10.00 p.m. up Paddy (a service officially known as 'The Northern Irishman') for London Euston. To roaring exhaust and shrieking whistles the two locomotives gave those present on that sad night an unforgettable ride across a dark, mist-shrouded countryside with the townsfolk of Newton Stewart and Castle Douglas standing six deep at the lineside. Despite the drinking of several farewell toasts (or maybe because of them!) arrival at Dumfries, where the pilot loco was detached, was sixteen minutes early at 12.30 a.m. and from Carlisle the train was taken forward by Britannia Pacific No. 70022.

Six wayside stations on the former Caledonian main line had been closed in 1960 (those on the former G&SW route survived until 1965) except for Beattock, which did not close until 1972, and Lockerbie, which still maintains a precarious existence. However, a small renaissance has taken place on the Nith Valley route with the reopening of the stations at Sanquhar and Gretna Green.

Undoubtedly the finest locomotives ever to operate on the West Coast main line were the Coronation Class Pacifics introduced by the LMS in 1937. Photographed on 29 July 1961, No. 46232, 'Duchess of Montrose', restarts a 9.05 a.m. relief train from Blackpool to Dundee West at Beattock Station with a 2-6-4T as banker for the ten mile climb to Beattock Summit.

The ten mile Beattock bank, starting at a gradient of 1 in 88 which increased to 1 in 74 before the 1,015 foot summit, posed severe operational problems in steam days and, with locomotives and staff constantly required for the banking of trains, resulted in a dedicated and close-knit railway community. Beattock bank was also a Mecca for photographers and at the end of the annual Glasgow Fair fortnight (particularly when this coincided with the English August bank holiday weekend) as many as ten extra trains were superimposed on an already augmented summer Saturday timetable of fifteen trains (usually there were nine). Photographed on 30 July 1960, Black Five No. 45099 leaves Beattock Station with a down relief.

Of necessity Beattock had a locomotive depot from the earliest days of the Caledonian Railway. For many years its allocation comprised ten or so 0-4-4Ts, but by the 1950s more modern 2-6-4Ts were being drafted in such as Nos. 42214 and 42239, seen here in this view from 4 August 1962. The banking engines waited in a loop on the down side of the line, at the south end of the station, to buffer up with northbound trains requiring assistance, and as each banker returned from the summit it trailed onto the others waiting in the loop.

Left: The earlier, parallel boiler LMS 2-6-4Ts were occasionally employed on the Beattock bank and on 29 July 1961 No. 42320 had been borrowed from Carlisle (Kingmoor) shed to augment the resident bankers on a day of exceptionally heavy traffic. It was photographed at the start of the bank, assisting a pair of Black Fives on the 9.15 a.m. Liverpool to Glasgow train.

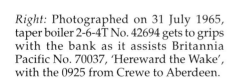

Right: Photographed on 31 July 1965, taper boiler 2-6-4T No. 42694 gets to grips with the bank as it assists Britannia Pacific No. 70037, 'Hereward the Wake', with the 0925 from Crewe to Aberdeen.

Standard class 4MT 2-6-0 No. 76104 being coaled at Beattock shed on 29 April 1967, prior to a final spell of duty as a banker. This was the last day of Scottish Region steam working and also banking that day were a pair of Black Fives. The depot was officially closed on and from 1 May, although it was utilised as a diesel stabling point for a few more years. Steam vanished entirely from Dumfries and Galloway on 31 December 1967 with the closure of Kingmoor depot at Carlisle.

'Beattock for Moffat' was the title of a short story by the Scottish writer and traveller R.B. Cunninghame Graham. However, this service ceased from 4 December 1954 with the closure of the Moffat branch to passengers. The town's provost made a speech before the departure of the last train and a wreath was placed on the locomotive by the local beauty queen. Among the passengers were two who had been on the first train when the branch opened in 1883. This photograph was taken on the last day and shows 0-4-4T No. 55232 of Caledonian Railway design in the dock platform at Beattock with the 1.10 p.m. for Moffat.

A seemingly timeless scene as 0-4-4T No. 55232 waits to propel its single coach from Moffat to Beattock on the afternoon of 4 December 1954. However, time was running out for the Moffat branch and that evening No. 55232 made the two mile, five minute journey for the last time.

Patriot 4-6-0 No. 45517 pulls out of Beattock Station with a 9.30 a.m. relief train from Southport to Glasgow Central on 29 July 1961 with a 2-6-4T assisting at the rear. The Patriots dated from the early 1930s, several being rebuilt in later years with new boilers which considerably altered their appearance.

Twelve minutes later and No. 45517 is passing Greskine, halfway up the bank, where there was a signal box and siding.

Another view at Greskine with Black Five No. 44974 on a northbound military special from Leeds to Stirling on 13 July 1963. Unusually, it was running ten minutes early.

Two miles short of the summit and Jubilee 4-6-0 No. 45578, 'United Provinces', is going well as it passes Harthope with the 9.15 a.m. from Liverpool to Glasgow Central on 13 July 1963. In the background, on the right, are Harthope Cottages and the viaduct spanning the A74 road.

Standard class 6 Pacific No. 72005, 'Clan Macgregor', tops Beattock bank on 1 August 1964 with a parcels train from Carlisle to Perth. Banking assistance was not required on this occasion as the load was within that laid down for this type of locomotive.

Coronation Pacific No. 46226, 'Duchess of Norfolk', passes Beattock Summit with the 7.35 a.m. summer Saturday train from Aberdeen to Manchester. On the left 2-6-4T No. 42239 waits to return to Beattock Station with the one coach staff train which picked up and set down at the several railway cottages en route, being used not only by signalmen and permanent way staff but also by their wives for shopping trips. It was known locally as 'The Siege', although the origin of the name is obscure; possibly it related in some way to the Boer War. The photograph was taken on a fine day, 4 August 1962, but the summit is a bleak spot in winter and the fence seen on the right was built to protect the line from drifting snow.

Photographed on Glasgow Fair Saturday, 13 July 1963, Black Five No. 45484 approaches Beattock Summit on the 1 in 99 northbound ascent from Elvanfoot, hauling a 10.30 a.m. relief train from Glasgow Central to Birmingham. The scene is much changed today with electrification of the railway, resiting of the M74 and reforestation.

From Elvanfoot Station in Lanarkshire, the Leadhills & Wanlockhead Light Railway, opened by the Caledonian Railway in 1901, terminated at Wanlockhead in Dumfriesshire. This photograph, taken on 1 August 1964, shows the start of the Light Railway, on the right, surviving as a head shunt, although the line had been closed on the last day of 1938. Jubilee 4-6-0 No. 45600, 'Bermuda', is passing on the main line with the 9.10 a.m. train from Southport to Glasgow Central. A two foot gauge tourist railway now operates between Leadhills and Wanlockhead.

From Wanlockhead, a ten mile trip through the Lowther Hills as the crow flies would bring one to the former G&SW main line. This company planned to serve the lead mines by means of a steeply graded branch, but this never materialised. On 27 July 1963 Black Five No. 45010 had passed Kirkconnel with a lengthy freight train and was photographed going downhill on the falling grades in the Nith Valley.

A five minutes journey would have brought No. 45010 to Sanquhar where, on the same day, I photographed standard class 5 No. 73100 leaving with the 6.10 p.m. from Carlisle to Glasgow St Enoch. The brickworks had been closed by this date and the station followed suit in 1965, being reopened as an unstaffed halt in 1994.

We last saw No. 49, 'Gordon Highlander', upon its arrival in Lockerbie on 13 June 1959 with the Stephenson Locomotive Society 'Golden Jubilee Special' from Glasgow. It then reached Dumfries by way of the former Lochmaben Railway, which had been closed to passengers in 1952, where it is seen here at platform one awaiting departure for Glasgow St Enoch. A Jubilee is leaving from platform three with a relief to the down 'Thames–Clyde Express' from London St Pancras. No. 49 now resides at the Glasgow Museum of Transport.

Class 2P 4-4-0 No. 40614, acting as station pilot at Dumfries on 13 June 1959. Although of Midland Railway origin and built at Derby by the LMS (which took over the Midland) in the late 1920s, these locomotives became synonymous with the G&SW.

Dumfries Station, looking north, photographed on 13 June 1959 with Black Five No. 45169 occupying the centre road with an up parcels train. The down platform and building, on the left, had formed the single long platform of the 1859 'new' station. The previous station, opened in 1849 to replace a temporary station in use in 1848, had been at the Annan Road.

G&SW locomotives did not long survive the railway grouping of 1923 and their replacements included not only LMS designs, but also former Caledonian types as shown in this 13 June 1959 photograph of class 2F 0-6-0 No. 57302 (the Caledonian's standard goods locomotive design) and class 3F 0-6-0 No. 57622 (Caledonian 812 class) at Dumfries shed.

More Caledonian locomotives at Dumfries on 13 June 1959. Class 3F No. 57601 had been built in 1900 while class 2F No. 57378 – which had been disfigured by a stovepipe chimney by the time of the photograph – was very much its senior as it was of a design which dated back to 1883.

Black Five No. 45469 at Dumfries with the last ever departure over the Port Road, the 6.20 p.m. to Stranraer Harbour, on 12 June 1965.

Black Five No. 45480, coming off the Port Road at Dumfries with a freight from Stranraer on 15 August 1964.

Standard 4MT 2-6-4T No. 80119, calling at Dalbeattie with the 3.50 p.m. from Stranraer Town to Dumfries on 10 April 1965.

Several of the compound 4-4-0s built by the LMS for main line work, but soon found to be underpowered, finished their days on the Port Road. On 29 October 1955 No. 41131 was at Castle Douglas with the 10.58 a.m. from Stranraer Town to Dumfries. It was scrapped early in 1958.

Ten BR class 6 Pacifics, bearing the names of Scottish clans, entered service during 1952 with five being allocated to Carlisle (Kingmoor) Motive Power Depot where they worked a locomotive diagram involving the Euston to Stranraer sleeper from Carlisle, the 11.44 a.m. Stranraer to Glasgow St Enoch returning with the 5.10 p.m., and then the Euston train back to Carlisle. They also appeared on the Newcastle to Stranraer boat trains and No. 72007, 'Clan Mackintosh', was photographed on 8 July 1961 at Castle Douglas with the 9.00 a.m. from Newcastle, having taken over the train at Carlisle.

Castle Douglas, reached by the G&SW in 1859, was junction for the Kirkcudbright branch which opened in 1864. Photographed on 8 July 1961, standard class 4MT 2-6-0 No. 76072 has curved away from Bridge of Dee and is approaching Castle Douglas with the 12.22 p.m. train from Kirkcudbright.

Photographed on 10 April 1965, one of No. 76072's sister locomotives, No. 76073, arrives punctually at Kirkcudbright at 3.48 p.m. with the 2.50 p.m. from Dumfries. The branch was closed three weeks later.

Right: From Castle Douglas the first station on the Portpatrick Railway was at Crossmichael and Black Five No. 45480 was photographed there on 8 July 1961, heading the 3.40 p.m. from Stranraer Town to Dumfries.

Left: The small single-platform station at Parton was adjacent to the River Dee. Photographed on 8 July 1961, Black Five No. 44885 is leaving with the 2.50 p.m. from Dumfries to Stranraer Town.

Lonely Loch Skerrow Halt comprised a crossing loop, signal box and water tank, along with short wooden platforms for railway staff, their families, and also anglers bound for the loch which had no road access. Photographed on 19 September 1964, the 3.50 p.m. from Stranraer Town to Dumfries is headed by Black Five No. 45471.

Gatehouse-of-Fleet Station was situated in hill country some six miles north of the small town and at the 495 foot summit of the line. Closed in December 1949, it was reopened six months later for just three trains per week and on 18 July 1964 Black Five No. 45460 was arriving with the 6.15 p.m. from Dumfries to Stranraer. The footplate crew are picking up the tablet from the signalman which authorised entry to the next single line section.

As the 3.35 p.m. from Stranraer Town to Dumfries ran into Creetown on 12 June 1965, the last day of service, the fireman of class 4MT 2-6-0 No. 76074 gave up the tablet for the single line from Newton Stewart and collected that for the section to Gatehouse-of-Fleet.

The Wigtownshire Railway from Newton Stewart to Whithorn was opened in 1877 and closed to passengers in 1950. On 15 April 1963 veteran Caledonian Jumbo 0-6-0 No. 57375 worked a 'Scottish Rambler' railtour over the branch and was photographed storming up the 1 in 67 grade past the former site of Kirkinner Station. Freight traffic to Whithorn ended in 1964.

The railtour over the Whithorn branch included a side trip from Millside to Garlieston. This small tidal harbour on Wigtown Bay was reached by rail in 1876 and had a meagre passenger service until 1903, thereafter seeing only an occasional Isle of Man boat train and a twice weekly freight. By the time of the tour passenger coaches were no longer permitted over the dilapidated one mile branch, although a train of open wagons was assembled for the tour participants. Fortunately, the weather was fine and the photograph shows the train being propelled back to Millisle by No. 57375.

Class 6 Pacific No. 72008, 'Clan Macleod', hurries through Dunragit with a 6.20 a.m. military special from Woodburn, Northumberland, to Stranraer Harbour on 29 May 1965. The three mile section from Dunragit to Castle Kennedy was converted to double track because of heavy wartime traffic.

Dunragit again on 29 May 1965, but looking in the opposite direction and seen from the signal box. Black Five No. 45363 is passing with a freight from Stranraer to Dumfries.

Returning weekenders wait at Dunragit to board the 3.45 p.m. service from Stranraer Town to Dumfries, headed by Black Five No. 44995, on Fair Monday, 15 July 1957.

Stranraer became a terminus upon the closure of Portpatrick in 1950 and received the suffix 'Town' in 1953 to distinguish it from the station at the harbour. It was photographed on 17 April 1954 with Black Five No. 45432 awaiting departure with the 3.40 p.m. to Dumfries. A former Caledonian Railway 0-4-4T, which was acting as station pilot, simmers in the background. Closure took place in March 1966, with passengers having to use the inconveniently situated harbour station which remains open.

Stranraer Motive Power Depot comprised a hotchpotch collection of elderly sheds, variously referred to as Joint, Caledonian and Girvan, together with an erecting shop where, in Portpatrick & Wigtownshire Railway days, locomotives had been dismantled for repair and overhaul and then re-erected. As evening shadows lengthened on 15 April 1963, class 6 Pacific No. 72006, 'Clan Mackenzie', Class 2MT 2-6-0 No. 46467 and Black Five No. 44795 were lined up outside the Joint shed. The depot closed in October 1966 when the 'Euston Paddy', diverted via Ayr upon closure of the Port Road, ceased to be steam hauled.

The T.S. *Caledonian Princess* leaving Stranraer on the 2.30 p.m. sailing for Larne on 7 September 1964. Following upon the tragic sinking early in 1953 of the diesel powered car ferry *Princess Victoria*, the Stranraer/Larne passenger and mail service reverted to the 1931 built T.S. *Princess Margaret*. However, in the autumn of 1959 a new car ferry was ordered by the British Transport Commission from Wm. Denny & Bros. of Dumbarton and entered service in December 1961. This was the 3,600 ton *Caledonian Princess* which was driven by steam turbines. She proved an immediate success, but with new and larger vessels required for the increasing traffic, left Stranraer for the last time in the summer of 1971. Thereafter she sailed from Fishguard to Rosslare, Weymouth to the Channel Islands, and finally from Dover to Calais, before being withdrawn in 1981.

The Cairnryan Military Railway served a wartime emergency port on Loch Ryan, six miles north of Stranraer, both of which were brought fully into use during 1943. After the war the facilities were used by the shipbreaking firm of H.G. Pounds and housed a pair of industrial steam locomotives. Photographed on 16 December 1962, this is an 0-4-0 saddle tank, built by Andrew Barclay & Co. of Kilmarnock in 1945, which had come from Sheerness Dockyard in Kent. The other locomotive – an 0-6-0 pannier tank built in 1940 by W.G. Bagnall Ltd of Stafford – had previously been at Rosyth Dockyard and both were eventually scrapped on site. Cairnryan is now a ferry port.

The Girvan & Portpatrick Railway (which became the Ayrshire & Wigtownshire in 1887 before being vested in the G&SW in 1892) joined the line from Dumfries at Challoch Junction and its steeply graded and tortuous single track now provides the sole rail access to Stranraer. On 29 May 1965 Black Five No. 45127 and its pilot, class 4MT Mogul No. 76112, were beginning the long climb which would take them past New Luce and Glenwhilly stations to the summit at Chirmorie, sixteen and a half miles from Challoch and 690 feet above sea level. They were hauling empty coaches from Stranraer to Ayr.

The single track south of Girvan was taxed to capacity at summer weekends and on Fair Saturday, 18 July 1964, Crab 2-6-0 No. 42789 and Jubilee 4-6-0 No. 45658, 'Keyes', heading a 12.22 p.m. relief train from Glasgow St Enoch to Stranraer Town, waited for half an hour in the loop at New Luce to cross a northbound boat train. New Luce Station was closed in September of the following year.

Later that day No. 42789 returned from Stranraer, assisting Black Five No. 44992 with the empty stock of the 12.22 p.m. up, and is seen here on the bleak moors near Glenwhilly.

The seven mile Langholm branch left the Waverley Route at Riddings Junction in Cumberland and almost immediately crossed the Liddle Water into Dumfriesshire, hence its inclusion in this volume. There were intermediate stations at Canonbie and Gilknockie, and the latter is seen here on 10 September 1960 with a solitary passenger waiting to board the 6.32 p.m. from Langholm to Carlisle, the two coaches of which had Ivatt class 4MT 2-6-0 No. 43139 as motive power.